Queen Elizabeth II

JENNIFER ZEIGER

Children's Press®
An Imprint of Scholastic Inc.

Content Consultant
Arianne Chernock, PhD
Associate Professor of History
Boston University
Boston, Massachusetts

Library of Congress Cataloging-in Publication Data
Zeiger, Jennifer.
  Queen Elizabeth II / by Jennifer Zeiger.
    pages cm. — (A true book)
  Includes bibliographical references and index.
  Audience: Grades 4–6.
  ISBN 978-0-531-21599-9 (library binding) — ISBN 978-0-531-21761-0 (pbk.)
  1. Elizabeth II, Queen of Great Britain, 1926-—Juvenile literature. 2. Queens—Great Britain—
Biography—Juvenile literature. I. Title.
  DA590.Z45 2015
  941.085092—dc23[B]   2014044843

© 2016 Scholastic Inc.
All rights reserved. Published in 2016 by Children's Press, an imprint of Scholastic Inc. Published
simultaneously in Canada. Printed in China 62
SCHOLASTIC, CHILDREN'S PRESS, A TRUE BOOK™ and associated logos are trademarks and/or
registered trademarks of Scholastic Inc.
1 2 3 4 5 6 7 8 9 10 R 25 24 23 22 21 20 19 18 17 16

**Front cover: Queen Elizabeth II
in her coronation robes**

**Back cover: Elizabeth during the
Trooping of the Colour in 2014**

Find the Truth!

Everything you are about to read is true *except* for one of the sentences on this page.

Which one is **TRUE**?

T or F   Queen Elizabeth is married to
King Philip of the United Kingdom.

T or F   Queen Elizabeth served in the
military during World War II.

Find the answers in this book.

Contents

THE BIG TRUTH!

**Princess
Diana**

Prince William, Queen Elizabeth's grandson, was married in 2011.

4 A Modern Monarch

What changed in 2013 regarding inheritance of the British throne?.......................... **39**

Elizabeth's portrait has appeared on money in about 30 countries.

6

CHAPTER 1

A Princess Is Born

Early on April 21, 1926, a girl was born in London, England. She was not just any baby. Elizabeth Alexandra Mary was a princess. Her parents were Prince Albert and Elizabeth, Duke and Duchess of York. Her grandfather was King George V, the United Kingdom's ruling **monarch**. Princess Elizabeth's father was the king's second son. She was third in line for the throne, behind her uncle Edward and her father. Few expected she would be queen.

Princess Elizabeth was baptized in lace first worn by Queen Elizabeth I in the 16th century.

Little Lilibet

The Duke and Duchess of York were often away from home on official business. However, Princess Elizabeth was well loved and cared for. When learning to talk, she called herself Lilibet. This naturally became the family's nickname for her. She also developed a deep love of dogs and horses that would continue throughout her life. When she wasn't with her real horses, she pretended to ride or even be a pony.

Elizabeth Alexandra Mary was named after her mother, grandmother, and great-grandmother.

Elizabeth (left) stands with her mother (center) and sister at the Royal Lodge.

In 1930, the Yorks had a second daughter, Princess Margaret Rose. The family of four first lived in and around London. When Princess Elizabeth was six years old, they moved to the Royal Lodge. This mansion is located in Windsor Great Park near Windsor Castle, a home of the king. Elizabeth had her own miniature house on the grounds. It was called Y Bwthyn Bach, which is Welsh for "The Little House."

Sisters Margaret (left) and Elizabeth (right) study with their mother (center) nearby.

Elizabeth and Margaret led a quiet life at first. Their father was unlikely to become king because his older brother was meant to inherit the crown. As a result, the sisters were mostly kept out of the public eye. They played with cousins and the children of people who worked for the Yorks. Even "Grandpa England," the king, came to play. The sisters did not go to school. A **governess** provided most of their education.

The Year of Three Kings

Everything changed in 1936. After a long illness, King George V died on January 20. Elizabeth's uncle became King Edward VIII. But Edward had fallen in love with Wallis Simpson, an American woman. Government leaders disapproved of the match because Simpson had been married twice before. They forced Edward to choose between Simpson and his country. He chose Simpson, abdicating (leaving) his throne on December 10. Elizabeth's father was unexpectedly left to take the crown.

Edward VIII and Wallis Simpson became the Duke and Duchess of Windsor after Edward abdicated and they married.

King George VI holds the royal scepter (left) and orb (right), two symbols of the monarchy.

Rising to the Challenge

Prince Albert, Duke of York, officially became king on December 11, 1936. His **coronation** ceremony took place the following May. The new ruler wanted to identify himself with his father and inspire the nation's trust. With this in mind, Prince Albert took his father's name, becoming King George VI. Albert's wife, Duchess Elizabeth, became the **queen consort**. Their daughter Elizabeth was now heir to the throne.

If Princess Elizabeth had had any brothers, they would have been in line to the throne before her.

Beginnings

The royal family moved into Buckingham Palace in London, the nation's capital. The palace was also where the king's offices were located. Princess Elizabeth started studying law and the British constitution in preparation for being queen.

As the family settled in, conflict was brewing in Europe. Germany's Nazi leader, Adolf Hitler, was working to expand his country's power in Europe. Germany was building up its military. Many people feared a war would begin.

Buckingham Palace has been the London home of Britain's monarchs for nearly 200 years.

Prince Philip was 18 years old when he met Princess Elizabeth.

In England, the royal family continued with their lives. During a summer trip in 1939, the family stopped in the town of Dartmouth to visit the Royal Naval College there. A young cadet, Prince Philip of Greece and Denmark, was asked to entertain the young princesses. Charming and handsome, he caught the eye of 13-year-old Elizabeth. The two became friends. They wrote to each other often in the following years.

Smoke and dust from fires fill the air in London during a night of bombing.

Leaving London

World War II officially broke out in September 1939 when Germany invaded its neighbor, Poland. By May 1940, German troops reached as far east as France. France is just across the English Channel from the United Kingdom. It was too close for comfort. That month, the king and queen evacuated their daughters to Windsor Castle in the country. George VI and his wife stayed behind in London. In September, German planes began bombing the city.

A Show of Strength

One role of the British monarchy is being a symbol of strength. King George VI and his wife lived up to this task during World War II. German bombs hit Buckingham Palace nine times, often while the king and queen were inside. Yet they refused to abandon the capital. A king's speeches are also an inspiration for the British people, particularly during wartime. But George VI struggled with a severe stammer. With help from his wife and a speech therapist, he was able to address the public regularly throughout the war.

Doing One's Bit

The princesses' wartime location was a closely kept secret. All the public knew was that they were living "in the country." During this time, Princess Elizabeth began taking on responsibilities to prepare for becoming queen. In October 1940, she went on a radio show with her sister to give her first public speech. In 1944, when she was just 18 years old, she started taking over some of her father's official activities when he was busy.

In her first speech, Elizabeth (right) talked about children who had been evacuated from London and other areas because of the war.

Elizabeth is the only female member of British royalty ever to join the military.

Elizabeth also learned to drive, first a horse-drawn carriage, then a car. In 1945, when she was old enough, she joined the Women's Auxiliary Territorial Service. This is the women's branch of the British army. Elizabeth served as a driver, learning to drive and repair trucks. She never saw action, though. Not long after she completed her training, Germany surrendered.

Thousands of people gathered at Buckingham Palace to see the royal family wave from the balcony the day the war ended.

Big Announcements

The war in Europe officially ended in victory for the United Kingdom and its allies on May 8, 1945. Recovery after the war was slow. Thousands of people had died, and the bombings had caused a lot of destruction. However, life was not all grim. On July 10, 1947, the royal family announced that Princess Elizabeth would marry Prince Philip. Philip would give up his title of Prince of Greece and Denmark to become a British subject and adopted the last name Mountbatten.

Like everyone else at the time, Elizabeth had to collect coupons for the cloth for her wedding dress. Many everyday supplies were limited after the war, but the royal family still put together a large and beautiful wedding. It took place on November 20, 1947. Philip was given the titles of Duke of Edinburgh, Earl of Merioneth, and Baron of Greenwich.

Elizabeth and Philip pose for a photo together on their wedding day.

Changes

The newly married couple settled in Clarence House, near Buckingham Palace in London. They also spent time in Malta, an island in the Mediterranean Sea. Philip was stationed there with the navy. Apart from official visits to other countries, life was relatively quiet. Their first child, a son named Charles Philip Arthur George, was born in November 1948. He became second in line to the throne after Elizabeth. A daughter, Anne Elizabeth Alice Louise, was born two years later.

The young royal family sits together on the lawn at Clarence House. From left to right are Elizabeth, Charles, Anne, and Philip.

Royal guards stand by the casket of the late King George VI.

By the 1950s, King George VI's health was failing. In late 1951, he had an operation to treat lung cancer. While he recovered, Princess Elizabeth and her husband started on a world tour originally planned for the king. Back at home, George VI remained weak after his surgery. He died suddenly of a heart attack on February 6, 1952, while Elizabeth and Philip were in Kenya. Shocked to hear the news, they returned home immediately. At the age of 25, Elizabeth officially became queen.

The Queen and Parliament

The United Kingdom is a constitutional monarchy. This means that its constitution limits the power of the queen or king. Though Elizabeth is queen, she does not control the nation's laws. Most governing power lies in the hands of members of Parliament, who write the laws, and the prime minister.

Parliament is made up of two houses: the House of Lords and the House of Commons. According to tradition, Elizabeth is never allowed in the Commons chamber. In fact, no British monarch has set foot there since one king's entry sparked a civil war in the 17th century.

The queen opens Parliament each year with a speech. Because she is not allowed in the Commons chamber, she has to wait on her throne in the Lords chamber. A representative called Black Rod is sent down the hall to the Commons chamber to invite its members over. When he reaches the Commons chamber door, the Commons members slam the door loudly in his face. By tradition, Black Rod knocks on the door with a big staff. After he knocks three times, the Commons members open the door and follow him into the Lords chamber to hear the queen's speech.

Elizabeth sits in the Coronation Chair, which has been used in coronations since 1308.

CHAPTER 3

Family and Country

Queen Elizabeth II mourned her father during the first months of her reign and limited her activities. She returned to the public eye slowly, beginning by opening Parliament in November. Then on June 2, 1953, came a joyful occasion: her coronation. People filled London's streets, despite the day's heavy rain, to see Elizabeth's carriage. Millions more watched from their homes around the world, as her coronation was the first to be broadcast on television.

After Elizabeth became queen, her mother became known as the Queen Mother or the Queen Mum.

Elizabeth made sure to meet and talk with people during her travels.

Getting Started

Following tradition, the queen's husband became Philip, Prince Consort. Only a male ruling monarch could hold the title of "king," and Elizabeth was the official ruler.

After her coronation, the queen was off and running. In the winter of 1953, she and Prince Philip resumed the world tour they had started in 1952. They traveled through parts of Africa, Asia, the Caribbean, Australia, New Zealand, and other areas.

What's in the Box?

Every day except Christmas and Easter, Queen Elizabeth receives a series of bright red boxes. Her private secretaries deliver each box. Inside are official papers from Parliament, letters, policies and laws in need of approval, and other documents. Elizabeth reads each and every one. If any documents need her approval, she signs them. All of this information keeps her up-to-date on events in her country and around the world.

Queen Elizabeth made some changes to the British monarchy. One of the biggest was to remove much of the formality that surrounded the treatment of royalty. She got rid of rules about how people could interact with her. She and Prince Philip also started going on "walkabouts" in many of the places they visited. On these occasions, they walked through neighborhoods and met the people who lived there.

Timeline to Becoming Queen

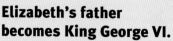

April 21, 1926
Princess Elizabeth Alexandra Mary is born.

December 11, 1936
Elizabeth's father becomes King George VI.

At Home

The royal family grew. In 1960, Andrew Albert Christian Edward was born. The birth made Elizabeth the first British monarch to have a child during her reign since her great-great-grandmother, Queen Victoria. Edward Anthony Richard Lewis was born in 1964. Then Elizabeth did something no British ruler had done before. Her daily activities were filmed. The resulting documentary aired on television in 1969 and captivated audiences.

November 20, 1947

Elizabeth marries Philip Mountbatten.

October 1940

Elizabeth gives her first public speech.

February 6, 1952

George VI dies; Elizabeth becomes queen.

31

Celebrations

In 1977, Elizabeth celebrated her 25th anniversary as queen. The yearlong celebration was called her Silver **Jubilee**. An estimated 10 million people across the United Kingdom took to the streets to cheer for Her Majesty that summer. Elizabeth and Philip also went on an extensive tour of the kingdom and the **Commonwealth**.

Elizabeth talks with members of the crowd gathered in south London to celebrate her Silver Jubilee.

The queen stayed calm throughout her 1981 birthday parade when a young man fired six blanks toward her.

Birthday festivities a few years later were less perfect. Though Elizabeth's real birthday is in April, the country celebrates the queen's birth each year on a sunny summer weekend. A big parade and special ceremony are held. During the birthday parade in June 1981, a young man fired six blanks at the queen. Her horse was spooked. But Elizabeth, unharmed, simply calmed the animal and continued the parade. The teenage shooter was quickly arrested.

Prince Charles (left) and Princess Diana (right) were often talked about in newspapers, in magazines, and on television.

The Horrible Year

The queen welcomed her first grandchildren in the late 1970s and 1980s. By 1990, Prince Charles, Princess Anne, and Prince Andrew each had two children. However, their family relations began to sour. In 1992, Anne and her husband divorced, and Andrew's marriage crumbled. Worse, Prince Charles and his wife, Diana, experienced a difficult separation. Diana was popular with the public, and the couple's struggles reflected badly on the royal family.

Then, in November of that same year, Windsor Castle caught fire. By the time firefighters put it out, the fire had caused roughly $90 million in damage. To raise funds for repairs, the queen opened her homes to the public. For the first time in history, anyone could pay for a tour of Buckingham Palace, Windsor Castle, or other royal houses. The fundraiser was a huge success, and the houses still open during certain seasons each year.

The queen called 1992 the *annus horribilis*, or the "horrible year."

The fire at Windsor Castle lasted about 15 hours. Some 250 firefighters worked to put it out.

The difficulties of 1992 were not limited to royalty. That year, the country was in a **recession**. Jobs were scarce. As the nation struggled, the queen took action. Taxes pay for public services such as roads and schools. They also support the royal family. Elizabeth had never had to pay taxes on her income. But in 1992, she announced that she would not only start paying taxes but also use more of her own money to pay for her expenses.

The recession meant many British people struggled to make enough money.

Queen Elizabeth holds the world record for most types of money to feature her face.

People left thousands of bouquets outside Buckingham Palace after Diana's death.

A Great Loss

Prince Charles and Diana divorced in 1996. One year later, Diana died in a car accident. People around the world mourned her. Because of the divorce, Queen Elizabeth at first did not acknowledge Diana's death officially by lowering the flag at Buckingham Palace. But the public disapproved so strongly that Elizabeth was forced to change her mind. Not long after, she and Philip visited the crowd standing outside the palace. They shook people's hands and gave and received comfort.

A Modern Monarch

Queen Elizabeth began the new millennium with both celebration and sorrow. The year 2002 marked her 50th year on the throne, her Golden Jubilee. However, two personal events cast a shadow over the celebrations. Princess Margaret Rose, the queen's sister, passed away in February. Shortly after, in March, the Queen's mother died at the age of 101.

Buckingham Palace held its first public concerts in 2002 as part of the queen's Golden Jubilee.

Prince William and Duchess Catherine kiss on the balcony of Buckingham Palace after their wedding.

A Growing Family

As the 21st century continued, Queen Elizabeth also experienced a lot of joy. Her first great-grandchild was born in 2010. In 2011, a huge royal wedding took place. Prince Charles's oldest son and heir, Prince William, married Catherine Middleton. The event was watched around the world. They had their first child, George Alexander Louis, in 2013. Prince George secured a third generation of kings for the United Kingdom. The couple's second child arrived in 2015.

Creating Change

In 2012, Elizabeth celebrated her 60th year as queen with her Diamond Jubilee. She has seen a lot of change during her rule. In 1982, she welcomed the first visit by a pope to the United Kingdom since the British monarchy broke from the Catholic Church in the 1500s. In 2011, she became the first British ruler to visit Ireland in 100 years. The United Kingdom and Ireland have long had a difficult and often violent relationship.

London's streets filled with people celebrating and waving the British flag during the Diamond Jubilee celebrations.

41

More big changes came to the monarchy in 2013. With the queen's support, Parliament passed a new law about who could inherit the throne. Before 2013, the crown first went to a ruler's oldest son, even if he had an older sister. If the ruler had no sons, the crown would pass to his or her oldest daughter. Under the new law, the oldest child takes the throne, no matter the gender.

The new inheritance law made changes for generations of royalty beginning with the children of Prince William and Duchess Catherine.

The queen does not have a passport or a driver's license.

Queen Elizabeth II's reign is among the longest in British history. By September 2015, she will have ruled longer than any monarch before her. She has lived through decades of ups and downs within her family and her country. Real and imagined moments from her life have been portrayed in films, television shows, paintings, and countless other works. With such an extensive reign, Elizabeth will go down in history as a strong and memorable leader. ★

Queen Elizabeth's full title: Elizabeth II, by the Grace of God, of the United Kingdom and Northern Ireland and of her other realms and territories Queen, Head of the Commonwealth, Defender of the Faith

Time and date Elizabeth was born: 2:40 a.m. on April 21, 1926

Number of countries Elizabeth has visited as queen: 116

Number of letters Elizabeth receives each day: Between 200 and 300

Number of letters Elizabeth responded to as queen by 2012: About 3.5 million

Date Elizabeth sent her first Tweet: October 24, 2014

Did you find the truth?

(F) Queen Elizabeth is married to King Philip of the United Kingdom.

(T) Queen Elizabeth served in the military during World War II.

Resources

Books

Doak, Robin S. *Kate Middleton*. New York: Children's Press, 2016.

Parker, Victoria. *Queen Elizabeth II*. Chicago: Heinemann Library, 2012.

Visit this Scholastic Web site for more information on Queen Elizabeth:
★ www.factsfornow.scholastic.com
Enter the keywords **Queen Elizabeth**

Important Words

Commonwealth (KAH-muhn-welth) — the organization of nations that are led by the British monarchy but separate from the British government

coronation (kor-uh-NAY-shun) — the ceremony in which a king, queen, or other ruler is crowned

governess (GUHV-ur-ness) — a woman who is hired to teach children in their home

jubilee (JOO-buh-lee) — the celebration of an important event

monarch (MAH-nurk) — a person who rules a country, such as a king or a queen

monarchy (MAH-nur-kee) — a government in which the head of state is a king or queen

prime minister (PRIME MIN-uh-stur) — the person in charge of a government in many countries

queen consort (KWEEN KAHN-sort) — the title given to the wife of the king of the United Kingdom

recession (ri-SESH-uhn) — a time when business slows down and more workers than usual are unemployed

Index

Page numbers in **bold** indicate illustrations.

About the Author

Jennifer Zeiger graduated with a bachelor of arts degree from DePaul University, where she studied English and Religious Studies and earned highest honors. Since then, she has written and edited scores of books for young readers, covering a range of topics from firefighters to big cats to the war in Afghanistan. When not writing, editing, or reading, Zeiger trains in capoeira and takes care of her cats in Chicago, Illinois.